The triumph of manipulation
Lukács and the 21st Century

Giovanni Alves

The triumph of manipulation
Lukács and the 21st Century

Praxis International

PRAXIS INTERNATIONAL IS A BRAND OF THE PROJETO
EDITORIAL PRAXIS - BRAZIL - THE PUBLISHER OF RET -
(Rede de Estudos do Trabalho)
(www.estudosdotrabalho.net)

The Free Press is Underground Press

Editor: Prof. Dr. Giovanni Alves (UNESP)

ISBN 9-781312-462229

Summary

Introduction

Our reflection seeks to highlight the historical fact that manipulation became the essential characteristic of capitalism after the Second World War. In coining the term "manipulative capitalism", Gyorgy Lukács was a visionary. The adjective "manipulative" qualifies the fundamental nature of the global system of capital. Therefore, more important than qualifying global capitalism as "cognitive capitalism", "neoliberal capitalism" or "technological capitalism" or even "financial capitalism", the most appropriate way to criticize capital is to qualify it as manipulative capitalism , since it is from its essentially manipulative nature that the capitalist mode of production organizes today – more than ever – politics, work, subjectivity, culture, ideology and technology. Therefore, manipulation in an unprecedented dimension in human history organizes the reproduction of global capital.

Never has the power of ideology as manipulation acquired such material force. After the Second World War, the technological resources of mass media and mass (dis)information developed impressively . From television to the

Internet with social networks, such means of mass manipulation contributed to boost the cultural revolution of capital. In a historically unprecedented dimension, consumption and politics became objects of manipulation by capital. We cannot underestimate the power of the new informational technologies in leveraging the power of ideology and the manipulation of human subjectivity in the service of the interests of the profit system.

Lukács did not live to see the triumph of manipulation, but managed to envision it as an essential element of the new order of relative surplus value. Thus, we live in a profoundly ideological era in the sense of an era of manipulation that has acquired a sophisticated technological base that permeates not only the production and circulation of global capital, but the living totality of human existence.

Since the 1980s, neoliberalism has not only meant a revolution in the economy and capital policy (increase in labor productivity and production of relative surplus value). Neoliberal neocapitalism has been, above all, a very powerful permanent cultural-ideological revolution. The innovative feature of global capital is to operate the fusion of ideology with informational technology in a network, increasing the manipulation of the ethical-value core of social relations and human subjectivity (consciousness and social unconsciousness).

When dealing with Americanism and Fordism in the "Cadernos do Cárcere" in 1934, Antonio Gramsci discerned the new historical meaning of the class struggle. The dispute for cultural hegemony became the dispute for the future of human civilization. Manipulation has acquired such proportions that we imagine the end of the world, but not the end of capitalism as a mode of production of social life. Like Lukács, Herbert Marcuse in 1966 dealt with the closure of the political and locutionary universe of affluent capitalism after the Second World War: the one-dimensional society or the one-dimensional man. Marcuse cultivated a pessimistic view of the future of industrial societies. In 1972, Ernest Mandel would title chapter 16 of his classic book "Late Capitalism", "Ideology in the Phase of Late Capitalism". Mandel – like Marcuse – criticized the ideology of technological rationality. Indeed, since the end of the Second World War, the problem of the critique of ideology has been the classic source of concern for the first generations of the Frankfurt Institute for Social Research) - at least Adorno, Horkheimer, Marcuse and Habermas. At the dawn of global capitalism (1989), István Mészáros published a seminal book: The power of ideology . Deep down, the ideological -technological mutation of late post-World War II capitalism changed the form of class struggle – including ideology and politics , and even the form of war – from the "war of movement" to the "war of movement". of position" (Gramsci); or even, from "conventional warfare" (military) to "hybrid warfare" (geoeconomic, geopolitical and techno-cultural).

It was not just a matter of ideology, an ineminable component of social life and the human development of men. The power of global capital acquired the sociometabolic density of manipulation as ideological processes of subjectivation and (de)formation of social consciousness leveraged through technological processes. Platform capitalism is not just a mode of technological organization of capital, but an ideological form constrained by manipulation. It is not just a question of ideological processes per se, but processes of deformation of the social subject capable of constructing "worldviews" parallel to the effective socio-historical reality . We thus have "ideological mechanisms" of a global nature as powerful as military artifacts themselves.

In the era of capital's structural crisis, the power of ideology as manipulation of the masses became fundamental for the reproduction of the dominant system. What is decisive is the superior scale of the ideological operation that has taken on a qualitatively new form in view of the global territory of the struggle for power. Ideology became manipulation thickened by capital's complex of contradictions. The material determinations of production and reproduction of the profit system; the accelerated speed of circulation of ideas and goods; the interconnected circuits of human exchanges, the cumulative movement of the "metabolic fracture" between capital and nature – in short, the "globalization" of the civilization of capital, produces unprecedented forms of historical becoming, operates qualitatively new leaps in terms of social dynamics. In fact, the complex movement of the globe of capital, fractured by the hegemonic disputes between its interstate political fractions (each one of them, in possession of nuclear power), has operated in the last decades of global capitalism, leaps and discontinuities that require critical thinking to re-elaborate high-level categories. It was in this sense that Lukács signaled with the "renaissance of Marxism" capable of being the historical critique of our time.

With global capitalism, alienation, estrangement and fetishism as a form of capital's social objectivity acquire unprecedented and qualitatively new dimensions, in view of capital's structural crisis. As Lukács pointed out in one of his interviews from the 1960s, "in terms of universal history, we are on the threshold of a world crisis". The idea of world crisis meant the structural crisis of capital that has characterized at least the last fifty years of capitalist decline (twilight capitalism). There is something new in the reign of capital – and it has gone rotten. It is not a mere replacement of structural forms of being alienated from the capitalist mode of production, but qualitatively new leaps in the sphere of capitalist social being that exacerbated alienation, estrangement and fetishism, and therefore, the power of ideology as manipulation. Thus, the critical elaboration from the thought of Karl Marx, is more necessary than ever - but not enough. This is what Marxists need to understand if they want to revive Marxism beyond the dogmatic and sectarian readings of the Marxian legacy.

Therefore, global capitalism, of a neoliberal, financialized and flexible nature, gave rise to the "tiredness society" and with it, the "neoliberal subject" and the new Reason of the world. Strictly speaking, the neoliberal subject is a non--subject. The meaning of capitalist ideology as manipulation has changed to the extent that it has at its core the dismantling of the modern subject capable of class consciousness. This is how "class desubjectivation" operated. The cultural revolution of neoliberalism reinforced the values of individualism and competition between people. The logic of the market has penetrated into the souls of men and women. The productive restructuring of capital and the precariousness of work assumed not only the character of technological-organizational innovation, but fundamentally an ideological offensive characterized by the "capture of the subjectivity" of living labor by the fetish-values of capital. Manipulation deepened generational cleavages and the movement of ideology as manipulation cultivated the fragment and the difference to, from there, reinforce particularism. The crassing identitarianism in the postmodern worldview is the prime example of the particularism that reduces class identities to fragments of self-absorbed people . The neoliberal non-subject has lost sight of the transcendence of the mercantile-capitalist order. The ideology of capital operated by manipulation effectively produced the subjectivation space of social barbarism.

In summary: the link between ideology as manipulation, deepening estrangement and social barbarism is intensely flagrant. This is what we present, in an essayistic way, in this small book on the actuality of Lukács's living thought. More than ever, it has become necessary to bring Lukacs's philosophical reflection closer to the historical and social problems of the 21st century. The paralysis of the dialectical imagination by the academicist appropriation of Lukács' legacy is tragic. Perhaps it was an expression of the debacle of the communist labor movement and of traditional Marxism. But, the 21st century may be the historic time of the renaissance of Marxism. It is necessary to revive Lukács' Marxism in deep dialogue with the human sciences that discuss the problem of our historical time. It is necessary to go beyond philosophy in the scholastic or academicist sense. The critique of capital is strengthened by going beyond the intellectual division of labor imposed by the university system. It is not a matter of mere interdisciplinarity (or transdisciplinarity), but rather the rescue of the historical-materialist sense of the critique of the social totality of capital.

The structural crisis of capital exhausted the heuristic effectiveness of the division of the particular sciences of man. The ontology of the social being and the understanding of the categories of work, ideology, social reproduction and estrangement, require a categorical elaboration of greater concreteness, with the incorporation to the critical-reflexive agenda of the social being, of the historical discussion of the phenomena of manipulation and barbarism social linkages with the study of capital production (and repro-duction) movements from the perspective of the critique of political economy and the critique of politics and bourgeois subjectivity.

Lukacsian ontological thought acquire greater scope with the confluence between the fundamen-tal crisis of the capitalist mode of production and the metabolic crisis of capital. On the one hand, the economic crisis (financial crises and specula-tive bubbles) and the geopolitics of capital (US imperialism); and, on the other hand, the explana-tion of the capital's metabolic contradictions that manifest themselves – for example – in ecological transitions (global warming and climate change); epidemiological transition (the new era of epide-mics and pandemics that slaughter the body and mind of living work); and demographic transition (global population ageing).

The complex of capital contradictions expo-sed by the metabolic fracture between capital and Nature (including living labor) evolved with the profound mutation of the technological base (the Fourth Industrial Revolution). The world of work as a social totality (the class perspective) is being irremediably permeated by global contradictions, interconnected and intertwined in a complex of social complexes. As world-historical individuals, the infranational perspective is inadequate for the true resolution of human problems in the 21st century.

Faced with the explicitness of the absolute limits of the capital appreciation process, the movement of the profit system manifests in an exacerbated way - more than ever - its necrophilic character. The movement of capital not only exploits and devalues the human labor force, but operates the movement of destruction of surplus population of living labor.

The triumph of manipulation is the triumph of senile capitalism that reached its peak with the 2020 pandemic and the war in Ukraine. This is what we witness in the last decades of neoliberal capitalism. And more than that – it is the catastrophic triumph of neoliberal capitalism that proves to be incapable of futurity. It is not a matter of imagining post-neoliberal capitalism because it does not exist. The capitalist mode of production has historically failed to solve the burning problems of the human species in the higher stage of the civilizing process. Perhaps in the course of the 21st century, the historical necessity of socialism may impose itself on the contingent consciousness of the masses still deluded by the politicism of senile liberal democracy.

From a theoretical-practical point of view, it has never been so important to criticize ideology as a manipulation of capital from a perspective of social totality. The critique of political economy is a necessity for critical thinking – if it wants to prosper. Ideology as manipulation also implies the manipulation (and degradation) of academic intelligence "captured" by neopositivism and postmodernism. Academicism, careerism and bureaucratization of the academic spirit are evils of our historical time.

Finally, financialized global capitalism, highly technologized and historically senile, thus became incapable of carrying out the civilizing process. The problems of senile capitalism are global problems demanding from our theoretical-critical apparatus a perspective of the historical materiality of the social totality. The various global problems are interrelated in a historically unprecedented way, operating a qualitatively new leap that tells us that we live in a radical time of crisis in the civilization of capital.

1

The presence of Lukács

In the last decade of his life (1961-1971), György Lukács closely followed what we can consider to be the beginnings of the new historical temporality opened with the structural crisis of capital, or even, the crisis of the historical rise phase of manipulative capitalism, begun shortly after the end of the Second World War in 1945. Lukács was aware (in 1969) that "we were on the threshold of a profound world crisis". The deep crisis of the global capital system had as its main historical landmark, the first global recession after 1945 (1973-1975). It was the culmination of a crisis process that began in the mid-1960s.

The great crisis boosted the following decades. the restructuring fury of capital with the deep (and wide) capitalist reaction in the most diverse spheres of social life that has persisted for more than half a century. We can characterize the new historical temporality of global capital by the productive restructuring (technological, organizational and territorial), which had profound impacts on the morphology of the working class; the neoliberal policies of work flexibilization with the degradation of wage contracting; and the increase in mass unemployment and the creation of a new and precarious world of work. In addition, the crisis of capital's hegemony in production and social reproduction meant that, from the 1970s onwards, the system boosted a true "cultural revolution" with postmodernism and the spread of neoliberal values. The mutation of capital's global order gained momentum with the collapse of socialist experiences in Eastern Europe and the USSR; the crisis of the socialist and communist parties and the collapse of class unionism. The new historical temporality of manipulative capitalism opened up, global capitalism as we call it the late historical phase of manipulative capitalism (Alves, 2018).

Capital's new neoliberal global order is essentially characterized by the deepening and triumph of manipulation as perceived by Lukács in the mid-1960s. The informational revolution (Lojkine , 1995); and the creation of the Internet and social networks in the 2010s, in addition to the proliferation of smartphones and the empire of information and communication technology corporations, deepened manipulation in everyday life to an unprecedented extent (work, consumption, politics). For at least fifty years (1970-2020), the triumph of manipulation represented the deepening of commodity fetishism and estrangement in social life, consummating itself in the sociometabolism of barbarism (Alves, 2011). In Lukács' interviews from the 1960s, we have the elements that they see as a fundamental problem of the era of senile capitalism, the intensification and amplitude of manipulation and the deepening of the phenomenon of estrangement as conceived by Lukács. Accompanying the master, István Mészáros realized the importance of the problem of alienation, publishing in 1970, "The theory of alienation in Marx" [Marx's theory of alienation , original title of the 1st. English edition by Merlin Press. A German book edition published in 1973 entitled *Der Entfremdungsbegriff Bei Marx*, published by List Verlag Munchen].

Lukács was a philosopher of many lives. The practice of criticism and self-criticism was part of his personality. He has never refused to assert the self-criticism of ideas he has championed in the past. Lukács spoke of the rebirth of Marxism.

But his own life was one of rebirth, criticism and self-criticism. Lukács categorically observed in 1966: "I started my real work at the age of seventy" (Lukács, 2020: 29) This is why we designate the "last Lukács" as the Lukács from 1955 to 1971. own intellectual-philosophical trajectory like Lukács. He was a man of many lives that represented his constant theoretical-critical self-improvement. He went through different historical conjunctures in the 20th century and knew how to reflect on them with passion for dialectical reason, not fearing self-criticism (which radically differentiated him from the Marxists of the 20th century, many of them imprisoned in Marxist dogma). Marxism's worst mistake was to renounce criticism and self-criticism . Stalinism represented the greatest degradation of Marxism in the 20th century. The response to Lucien Goldman was sincere and blunt to the French philosopher who was too attached to HCC, forgetting all the later development of Lukács (Tertulian , 2008:292) [emphasis added]. Goldmann never ceased to glorify himself as "the greatest thinker of the 20th century", but exclusively for the contribution brought by his youthful works. In a letter, Lukács gave him a blunt reply in a letter sent on October 1, 1959 and which is a sample of the epistolary style lukácsiano : "If

I had died around 1924, and if my immutable soul had looked at your literary activity from the beyond, it would be full of joy and true gratitude for occupying you so intensely with my youthful works. But since I am not dead, and for thirty-four years I have created what must be called my life's work, and since, in short, for you, this work does not exist at all, it is difficult for me, as living being, whose interests are evidently directed towards its own present activity, take your considerations into account." (Lukács, 2020:292)

At first, we will demonstrate that the last Lukács (1955-1971) predicted the new era of manipulative capitalism as it manifested itself in the peak (and crisis) of Fordist-Keynesian capitalism after the Second World War. Based on excerpts from his interviews organized by Ronaldo Vielmi Fortes in the book published by Boitempo editorial (2020), we will highlight the burning relevance of the late (and incomplete) reflections of the last Lukács. It was the deep (and wide) capitalist crisis of the 1970s that led to the formation and rise of global capitalism as we know it. A burning feature of global capitalism is the exacerbation of manipulation. In fact, after the death of Lukács in 1971, we see in the following decades of rise and crisis of global capitalism, the triumph of manipulation and the sociometabolism of barbarism as the fundamental trait of the global system of capital.

Then we will deal, in an introductory way, with the nature of manipulative capitalism and the deepening of estrangement as an ineliminable trait of exacerbation of the reactionary shock of capital, as verified in the following decades. Although Lukács did not perceive the debacle of the socialist experiences of Eastern Europe and the USSR and underestimated the capacity of the global system of capital – in this case, US capitalism – to react to its deep crisis as he saw it in the 1960s, the his perceptions on the need to renew Marxism (criticism of Stalinism, socialism as democratization of everyday life and the affirmation of the method of ontological Marxism capable of understanding the substantial changes of late capitalism, that is, the emergence of manipulative capitalism and its implications ethical-political and ideological).

2

The 1960s: The ideological crisis of capital

One of the burning themes of the various interviews given by old Lukács was the crisis of US hegemony, not only due to the exhaustion of the growth cycle of the economy of the central capitalist countries, but due to the irruption of the movement against the Vietnam War, the counterculture, the struggle of blacks for civil rights and for the social revolution, the student movement contesting the pillars of the bourgeois order as it was constituted in the immediate post-war period, the wars of national liberation in Africa. From the perspective of the totality of the world-system of capital, such events were indications of the profound general crisis of capitalism and, from Lukács's perspective, the bankruptcy of the ideology of the American way of life . In a 1968 interview, Lukács interpreted this as the ideological crisis of the system: "The ideologies formed in the determining capitalist countries, on the basis of the victory of 1945, entered, without exception, in crisis. This is clearly seen in the United States, where the dream of political and ideological 'American hegemony' after 1945, and the illusion regarding the American way of life, collapsed. Today, even more so, the Vietnam War and the enormous difficulties of integrating black people make it clear that this American ideology formed in 1945 is almost completely bankrupt (Lukács, 2020:43).

It is curious that Lukács believed in the impossibility of incorporating blacks into US capitalism (Lukács, 2020:198). The capitalist turn that took place in the 1970s, showed the strength of the American capitalist system in the ideological renewal aimed at incorporating them, as happened with the youth and women's movement, in the liberal perspective. This was one of the elements of the triumph of manipulation. But since 1966 at least, as Lukács' interviews show, he has observed signs of an establishment crisis . The social upheaval in the US and Western Europe indicated fractures in the order of late capitalism. In 1964, Herbert Marcuse published One-Dimensional Man: Studies in the ideology of Advanced Industrial Society (in Brazil, the book was entitled "The ideology of industrial society: The unidimensional man"). Marcuse highlighted the integration of the proletariat by industrial society, seeing in the student protest movement the new revolutionary subjects. However, unlike Marcuse, Lukács was critical of the intellectual and student protest movements against the system in the West. In a 1969 interview he observed: "Students and intellectuals have not yet produced a genuinely elaborate program. The program they produce in most cases is very naive. Young people, for example, often talk about the need to eliminate manipulation and make work a game. This would lead to the renewal of what [Charles] Fourier demanded at the beginning of the 19th century and what Marx mocked in the 1840s. manipulative" (Lukács, 2020:137). And he highlighted: "In terms of universal history, we are on the threshold of a world crisis. This period can last fifty years. This must be clarified once and for all, we must germinate in a historic time of crisis to be fully aware of this" (Lukács, 2020:137)

Lukács placed the problematic of the ideological crisis in the perspective of the class struggle.

To what extent could the socialist movement respond to the crisis? He said: "The ideology of the American way of life is collapsing with the Vietnam war, as well as internally, with the black issue. The situation is analogous in England and even elsewhere. It is about knowing to what extent we are capable of supplanting this ideology and presenting a new ideology " (Lukács, 2020:137) [emphasis added]. That is, would the countries of bureaucratic socialism have the capacity to present a new ideology that would compete for cultural hegemony in the West. Lukács highlighted the disastrous damage of Stalinism on the European workers' movement. A nostra res agitur – the feeling that, for example, what was happening in the Soviet Union and in the socialist countries was something decisive for the very lives of European workers (a feeling that existed in Europe right after the Russian Revolution of 1917), only could be recovered with the revitalization of socialist democracy.

In the Lukacsian perspective, the crisis of manipulative capitalism represented the ideological crisis. It was not a mere crisis of the capitalist economy (profitability crisis) as it "exploded" in the global recession of 1973-1975. It was a cultural crisis. Lukács pointed out that dissatisfaction with capitalism might or might not be harnessed by socialism. This was the question: "All those who are dissatisfied with capitalism, both economically and politically and culturally, instinctively turn to us for an intelligent answer to their problems. Now, if we give them a bureaucratic answer, born from a momentary tactical thought, or from the works of a supposed writer well considered by us, it is clear that the prestige of socialism diminishes and opinion is formed more and more in the West - among those who they do not defend capitalism, because they cannot defend it - that the fate of humanity is, in essence, hopeless, and unfortunately much has already been formed in this regard; neither capitalism nor socialism can provide an answer. That is why we have the serious responsibility of imperatively prescribing the path we must take". (Lukács, 2020:137)

The ruin of capitalism would not mean the triumph of socialism. This is what Lukács highlighted. If socialism did not present superior cultural products and the democratization of everyday life, it would not be able to respond to the dissatisfaction of the masses and bring youth closer to Marxism. The feeling of revolt would be diluted and the capital system could recompose itself in a new ideological offensive. This is what historically happened in the decades of formation and rise of global capitalism (1975-1991), when capital made a cultural revolution that represented the triumph of manipulation and the collapse of socialism, as happened with the end of Eastern Europe and the USSR.

According to Lukács in the 1970 interview, the first manifestations of the structural crisis of capital was the moment for the renewal of Marxism in the perspective of responding to the dissatisfaction of the masses. He said: "We are at the beginning of a revolutionary shock" (Lukács, 2020:191). The subjective factor was important, if not fundamental, even to calibrate the duration of the crisis. Mészáros called the crisis of the global system of capital the structural crisis of capital, which has persisted for at least fifty years (1970-2020). We consider global capitalism to be the historical form of the structural crisis of capital within which the contradictions of value "affected by negation" manifest themselves with ease (Alves, 2018).

The invasion of Czechoslovakia by the USSR in 1968 shattered Lukács's optimistic perspective on the revival of socialism. In the interview given in 1970 by the old Marxist philosopher to Franco Ferraroti, Lukács was tough on Marxism. "[...] we are still all Stalinists. Without a general theory of society and its moment, one cannot leave Stalinism." Marxism as the only general theory of society was closed. Lukács noted that Marxism, as a general theory of society and history, had come to a halt: "It closed down," he said. When provoked by Ferraroti, he was tougher: "[Marxism] no longer exists, it ended some time ago [...] there are no more theorists. There are only tacticians" (Lukács, 2020:207) – that is, those who put practice ahead of theory "and perhaps against it", as Stalin did.

In the set of interviews, Lukács emphatically emphasized the need for Marxists to go beyond fragments and create a Marxist theory of analysis of today's social phenomena (Lukács, 2003:78). This is the "concrete totality" perspective that since History and Class Consciousness: Studies in Marxist Dialectics (HCC) in 1923, Lukács has emphasized as being the Marxist perspective. Finally, this was not a mere critique of political economy, although it is itself the necessary condition for a materialist analysis of manipulative capitalism. The need for the new Capital is to interpret the new capitalism of the crisis, which is the need for the ideological struggle. The renaissance of Marx's theory and method would occur when we face a new Marxist theory of extended reproduction, encompassing, according to him, three complexes of problems:

Firstly, the genuine theoretical analysis of the extended reproduction theory presented in Book II of Capital , since according to Lukács (and Engels' confirmation), there are gaps, the description being fragmentary in nature. It is curious that Lukács makes reference to Book II, but not to Book III, where today the criticisms of those who say that Marx does not have a theory of the capitalist crisis are concentrated (Nozaki , 2021).

Secondly, Lukács pointed out that Karl Marx wrote Capital a hundred years ago (1967-1867), demanding from us an effective analysis of the capitalism that exists today: "This has not yet happened. I am neither an economist nor an expert on this subject, just allow me to point to an example: in Marx's time basically only heavy industry and some raw material industries were really capitalist. What was produced for consumption and for so-called services was almost entirely at the handicraft level. And when you read Marx's theories, you will see that evidently - this is not a caesura, as it could not be otherwise - they are based on the capitalism that really existed in his time" (Lukács, 2020:213).

Lukács pointed out in the mid-1960s that the service industry had become a major capitalist territory. But it is not just a matter of talking about a "consumer society". Economically, capitalism in pre-Marxist times was so-called heavy industry capitalism in the broadest sense, and the production of the means of consumption was largely in the hands of artisans. Lukács observed that this had two consequences : "One consequence was that, for capitalism, workers' consumption was something completely indifferent, since workers' consumption goods were bought from small artisans and non-capitalists , so that, for the capitalism, whether the worker earned x or 2x per week, from an economic point of view, this was completely indifferent. [Capital] accumulated by expropriating the small artisans, the artisans entered the factory, and that was the end of it. Meanwhile the process gradually took its course and the consumer goods industry became completely capitalist and even, as you can see everywhere, the so-called services, which 100 or 150 years ago had nothing to do with capitalism." (Lukács, 2020:174/175)

The Hungarian philosopher gave an example from his everyday life: "I don't know if you know - you're too young for this, I know -, the summer holidays in my youth consisted of renting part of a big house in a place with the owner of the big house and cook with a village cook, or spend the summer with the cooks themselves, who were taken to the workshops. Resort hotels were a rarity at that time. I do not say, then, that Carlsbad , Marienbad , etc. they had no hotels. But it is clear that, in fact, although more ridiculous, remote and climatic, naturally there was nothing in the villages that could be considered a hotel" (Lukács, 2020:175).

Finally, capitalism became the owner of the entire production industry, of the entire consumer goods industry and of all services. As a result, on the one hand, the ground for acquiring new workers has become much less. Craftsmen no longer exist, or there are only a minimal number: they had to perish to become workers in the factory. Thus, the extensive expansion of capitalism becomes more difficult, emphasizing an intensive expansion through the improvement of the means of production. And secondly, capitalism has come to take the worker seriously as a consumer. Therefore, all of capitalism has an interest – he said – "that wages increase and the working hour is reduced, because, in doing so, the worker becomes a better consumer, an issue that in the time when Marx lived did not even exist as a question" (Lukács was wrong to disregard that, given the crisis of profitability as manifested in the global recession of 1973-1975, the logic of late capitalism in its phase of historical decadence, did not allow maintaining the indexation of wages and labor productivity as occurred in Fordist-Keynesian capitalism). Therefore, the expansion of the consumer goods industry and most "services" was not a question of a mere quantitative extension of the sphere of influence of capitalism, but of qualitatively new changes directly related from an economic point of view to the consumption of the working class. The predominance of relative surplus value meant the expansion of reification (and estrangement) in social life (here is the reiteration of the "old" theme that Lukács addressed in HCC of 1923). He said: "Without going into details, allow me to As a consequence of this, the relative surplus-value, as a form of exploitation, ends up dominating the absolute surplus-value, since only this new guarantees the intensification of exploitation in the event of an increase in contemporary consumption (and free time) of workers. With that, however, capitalism does not cease to be capitalism. Marx wrote somewhere that only with the predominance of relative surplus value, the "real subsumption" of the economy could occur in capitalism" (Lukács, 2020:216).

It was with the dominance of services that social production in its entirety became capitalist.

Therefore, he noted, "it is no coincidence that so-called absolute surplus value became the dominant factor in capitalist exploitation at the time. Since global production has become capitalist - according to US statistics, there are more people employed in services today than in heavy industry - working class consumption is of the utmost importance for the functioning of global capital. But there are problems for global capital as worker consumption has become of paramount importance. He says: "[...] the total consumption of society represents a problem, because it raises the question that workers are considered consumers of capitalism. But capitalism can only solve this question in a purely marketing way".

Finally, for Lukács, capitalism encompasses, invests, understands very closely, even conditions, all aspects of life. The logic of capitalism tends to coincide with the very logic of the social process as such, expanding and involving all of social life: "From the partial capitalism of the last century we have moved to generalized capitalism. In this sense, far from being exhausted, it can be said that Marxism did not even begin. In any case, and paradoxes aside, it is necessary to complement Marxism; it is necessary to study what Marx did not study in depth." (Lukács, 2020:204)

What Lukács persistently reiterated was that today's capitalism, this in the 1960s, is, precisely as capitalism, something very different from the capitalism of Marx's time. We can say in the same way: 21st century capitalism is in precisely the same way, different from late capitalism in its historical rise phase (1945-1975). Lukacs's claim was to produce an analysis of capitalism that, with Marxist methods, precisely shows the specific characteristics of capitalism today. (p.159). Anyway, today we have a capitalist economy, but structured in a different way. And we must now subject all the categories that Marx established for capitalism in the 1880s to a new Marxist investigation. The need for ideological struggle makes it necessary to go beyond dogmatism. For Lukács, it is dogmatic Marxism that makes us wait for the outbreak of a new crisis like that of 1929. At the same time, it is necessary to confront the bourgeois theorists who say that capitalism no longer exists and that Marx's analysis is a document from the 19th century . He said: "Although I am not an economist, I think that this transformation can be fully explained with the help of the Marxist method" (p. 211). But Lukács warned that "economic reasons explain nothing. One must always be aware of the risk of mechanically interpreting Marxism.

The positivist interpretation of Marxism is a premise, political and philosophical, of opportunism and also of Stalinism." (p, 211).

Finally, thirdly, Lukács noted that a hundred years ago, Marx could examine the laws of reproduction of the social form of production only in capitalism. Today – says Lukács – we can ask whether, in addition to the certainly considerable number of common aspects existing in capitalist and socialist reproduction, there are not determinations that assert themselves in both social formations. Indeed, this deals with a very important theoretical problem; therefore, one should not hastily anticipate its results. So the renaissance of Marxism is this: "Examining exactly what the economic peculiarities of capitalism today are and then making the attitude towards capitalism depend on that analysis and not on the analyzes of eighty years ago." (p. 175) Lukács stressed the need to elaborate a general Marxist theory applied to current conditions – which is a collective task and not individual solitary thinkers: "There are new phenomena about which we have nothing to say". But, as we will see in the next citation, Lukács did not fail to make theoretical mistakes in the analysis of the political economy of late capitalism, overestimating, for example, the ability of late capitalism to overcome crises through consumption – at least as a mechanism of the economy. (this is an underconsumer bias that would characterize, for example, the Marxist political economy of Paul Baran and Paul Sweezy (see "Monopoly Capitalism: Essay on the American Economic and Social Order" [Monopoly capital: An essay on the american economical and social order], originally published in 1966 (Alves, 2018:130). It is curious that István Meszáros also incorporated, at the time, the analytical perception of Paul Baran and Paul Sweezy exposed in the book Monopoly capital (see Alves, 2018:128-129).

Despite the development of capitalism having undergone radical, qualitative changes, this did not mean that the law of value and the downward movement of the rate of profit could be disregarded as a determination of the capitalist crisis, putting in its place the increase in real indexed wages. the productivity rate (the consumption of the working class). He said: "I observe that Marxists wait for the great crisis of capitalism, but capitalism has not had a major crisis since that of 1929, because today capitalism has taken over all social life. I don't like to say it, but it's the truth. Mass consumption by workers has become very important as a means of eliminating the crises of capitalism . From the structural, objective market, endowed with an important social function, in many aspects revolutionary, as Marx and Engels knew it, compared to the idiocy of rural life and tradition in general, we pass to the manipulated market of this century. Our analysis stalled, capitalism continued to evolve. We stop with Lenin. After him there was no Marxism." (Lukács, 2020: 191).

The idea of manipulative capitalism as a consumer society has become a fertile idea as a movement of social reproduction through the ideology of the manipulated market. However, what explains the spread of manipulation as a social reproduction strategy is the surplus value production crisis. The discussion of the capitalist crisis became quite fertile from the 1970s onwards, which had not occurred since the 1920s with the thesis of capitalist collapse. Lukács confronted the "collapse theory", but did not offer a theory of crisis adequate to the era of structural crisis of capital that began with the crisis of late capitalism (the Trotskyist economist Ernest Mandel made a brilliant contribution in 1972, with the book " Late Capitalism"). But Lukács' emphasis is on the crisis of capitalist ideology and the form of capitalist crisis under the conditions of manipulative capitalism. That's what it's about. He does not discuss a critique of political economy, but a critique of capitalist reproduction through manipulation that has become a crucial element of the global system of capital. For example, by placing consumption and free time as elements of manipulative capitalism or of a more developed industrial society, as Marcuse would say, Lukacs refers to new forms of alienation. This is what interests the Hungarian philosopher, since ideology became crucial in the class struggle: "For example, over the course of the last century, the length of the working day was an important issue: it went from fourteen hours to thirteen, twelve, ten and so on. Today, the question itself is posed differently. It is not so much the length of the work week that is important; the important thing is to know and program what the workers will do during their famous «free time", what they consume, where they go... In the last century, in their projects and speculations, the capitalist never took into account the consumption capacity of the workers, because this was in fact quietly negligible. Capitalism was interested above all in base investment, in large-scale industry. Important sectors of collective life were indifferent to it. Today, capitalism is deeply interested in all social life, from women's boots to automobiles, from kitchen appliances to entertainment media... It's a qualitative change about which we know little [Lukács, 2020:215/216]

In the second part of the essay, we will deal with the new sociometabolic dynamics of manipulative capitalism based on structural changes in the capitalist mode of production. Our hypothesis is that the Hungarian philosopher managed to apprehend the manipulative nature of capital in its historical ascension stage. The point is that today we are witnessing manipulative capitalism in the stage of the structural crisis of capital, where the problem of manipulation becomes even more burning because of global capitalism. The idea of manipulative capitalism, much more fertile than that of industrial society or "one-dimensional man" (Marcuse), became the central axis of an analytical perception that is the very material presupposition of the need for ontology and the new Marxist ethics. Despite the importance of the economy from an ontological perspective, the fundamental dimension (and it has not always been so) is today, more than ever, the cultural dimension in the sense of the material field from which individuals make their ethical-moral choices in the face of alternatives. placed in a crisis situation. For this reason, the theme of estrangement for him was so crucial as it concerned the political struggle in conditions of structural crisis and profound manipulation of capital.

Lukács did not use the term "structural crisis", but "general crisis of capitalism". But he knew that the world crisis that manifested itself in the mid-1960s would not be just any cyclical crisis, but, according to him, could last for decades (Lukács, 2020:137). In fact, with the structural crisis of capital, the dynamics of the system would be that of "destructive production" (Mészáros, 2002:605). The emphasis on the "democratization of everyday life" as an intrinsic part of the criticism of Stalinism was not a mere " theoretical reduction " by Lukács, as José Paulo Netto supposes in the "Introduction" to the book "Socialism and democratization: Political writings (1956-1971)", by György Lukács (p.21/22), but a necessary element posed by the emergence of the struggle against manipulation that has everyday life as its root. Perhaps the old Lukács was, to a certain extent, optimistic about the possibility of restructuring bureaucratic socialism through economic reforms – and not only: he was emphatic in affirming the importance of the democratization of everyday life, because, without it, the restructuring of the economy was impossible (which, in fact, happened).

In his interviews after the invasion of Czechoslovakia in 1968, Lukács became more pessimistic about the possibility of reforming bureaucratic socialism. But, after the death of the old Hungarian philosopher in 1971, the triumph of manipulation would occur at the level of the global system of capital - not only with the persistence of Stalinism in countries of bureaucratic socialism, but with capitalist manipulation in politics (rotting of liberal democracy) and consumption (consumerism spread across the globe with the offensive of capital from liberal globalization). The prevalence of neoliberalism and the formation and rise of global capitalism, and soon after, the global crisis of 2008 and the deepening of the sociometabolism of barbarism, characterize the era of triumph of manipulation (1980-2020).

The triumph of manipulation acquired substance with social barbarism altering the terms of estrangement, not only the realm of consumerism and the manipulation of free time (the terms of historically ascending late capitalism), but the new forms of precariousness of life and work and the reduction of living time (otium) to working time . The issue of reducing working hours and free time has lost importance on the agenda of the labor movement's struggle. The logic of work flexibilization, the spread of the precariat and the new poverty with the spread of extreme forms of particularism (or estrangement) came into effect. More than ever, there is an urgent need for Marxism to give theoretical answers to the new historical time of social barbarism.

3

The Triumph of Manipulation and the Sociometabolism of Barbarism

In Part I of our essay, we saw that, in his last interviews (1966-1971), the reflections of the last Lukács were incisively focused on the critique of manipulation in the various spheres of human thought and activity. We will pause to carefully outline the theme of manipulation in the late capitalism era, in the 1965 interview given to the German intellectuals Hans Heinz Holz, Leo Kofler and Wolfgang Abendroth , originally published in Brazil, in the book "Conversando com Lukács" (Ed. Paz e Terra, 1965). Gyorgy Lukács called post-World War II capitalism "manipulative capitalism" (what Ernest Mandel called "late capitalism"). Indeed, under late capitalism, manipulation becomes an essential nexus of social metabolism, penetrating the various pores of everyday life. Manipulation became the structuring and structuring matrix of alienation in its intense and expanded form, thus contributing to the de-effectiveness of man's generic being. Lukács stated that, with the new socio-historical reality of manipulative capitalism, ontological investigations about the nature of alienation/estrangement become necessary, which cannot be reduced to that observed by Karl Marx and Friedrich Engels in the second half of the 19th century. At that time, industrial capitalism had not yet exposed manipulation as a trait of capital's sociometabolic conformation, which would only occur during the course of the 20th century, the century of capitalist modernization on a planetary scale.

In his 1965 interview, old Lukács noted that manipulative capitalism is a specific form of industrial capitalism. After the 1929 crisis, world capitalism underwent significant structural transformations that altered the social metabolism of capital. For example, the communist Antonio Gramsci, in the text "Americanism and Fordism" (1934), managed to apprehend the traits of the new capitalism through the concepts of "Americanism" and "Fordism", which express the new hegemonic cultural reality of the capitalism of the mass production, characterized not only by the new model of commodity production, but by the new organization of culture and intellectuals. For György Lukács, what emerged as a crucial element in terms of human praxis was the problem of manipulation, which he linked to the expansion of the world of goods, and consequently, to the presence of capitalist industrialization in our lives: "If we go back 80 or 100 years, to the time when Marx was working, we see that the means of production industry was, in its essence, largely organized on a capitalist scale; we can observe it in the textile industry, in the milling industry, in the sugar industry, which formed almost all the economic sectors of the great capitalist industry. Now, in the following eighty years, all consumption was absorbed by the capitalist process. I'm not just talking about the shoe industry, apparel ¬, etc.; It is very interesting that with all these refrigerators, washing machines, etc., even the domestic sphere is beginning to be dominated by industry. Even the so-called service sector becomes part of big capitalist industry. The semifeudal figure of the domestic servant of Marx's times becomes increasingly anachronistic and a system of capitalist services emerges. (Holz, Kofler and Abendroth, 1966: p.150).

A. COMMODITY MASS PRODUCTION, CONSUMPTION AND MANIPULATION

The capitalism of mass production, called "Fordist-Keynesian capitalism", is the capitalism of big industry, whose products-commodities invade the most diverse aspects of social life. The capitalist process occupied and filled the most diverse spaces of human consumption. The social world has become an immense collection of commodities. It was by emphasizing this feature of the bourgeois world that Karl Marx opened Chapter 1 of Book I of "Capital". He says: "The wealth of societies in which the capitalist mode of production dominates appears as an 'immense collection of goods' [...]" (Marx, 1996). Perhaps, in that simple Marxian observation, which the 20th century would exhaustively demonstrate, contained the problem of manipulation irremediably linked to the expansiveness of the commodity form that would impregnate the products of human labor.

To the extent that the commodity is not only use value, but also exchange value, the buying-selling relationship tends to involve men and women with the naturalized, and therefore fetishized, impositions of the market and the law of value. It was section 4 of chapter 1 of book I of "Capital", entitled "The commodity fetish and its secret" that inspired Lukács to address capitalist reification in his classic book History and Class Consciousness (1923). At that time, for the first time, a Marxist author addressed the implications of commodity fetishism on human thought and activity. The mass production of goods created the need for large apparatuses for the distribution and circulation of goods that encompass the entirety of social life. Under monopoly capitalism it becomes a veritable obsession to sell commodity products that are produced on a large scale. Large industry began to encompass and transform into a commodity product the most diverse aspects of social life, such as, for example, politics and leisure, which are impregnated by the commodity form. Lukács says: "Take a great machine builder or any other industrialist of Marx's time. Of course, its clientele was extremely limited, so that it could distribute its products without setting up a larger apparatus ¬. But, with the means of big industry, a product appeared for mass consumption (just think of products such as razor blades) that required a special apparatus to bring millions of razor blades to private consumers. I am convinced that the whole system of manipulation we are talking about arose from this need and then spread to society and politics as well. Now this mechanism dominates all expressions of social life, from presidential elections to the consumption of ties and cigarettes" ((Holz, Kofler and Abendroth, 1966: p.150)

In this way, Lukács linked the emergence of manipulation with the emergence of the society of mass consumption of goods (which Antonio Gramsci would deal with in "Americanism and Fordism") (Gramsci, 2001). Capital was forced to manipulate in order to be able to sell the commodity products and realize the surplus value contained in them. This is the burning feature of capital's new fetishized sociability.

The Lukácsian perspective is a historical--materialist perspective that takes into account the concrete totality of capital production (production, distribution, circulation and consumption). Manipulation originates from the enlarged and voracious movement of the mechanism of capital production. He says: " Now this mechanism dominates all expressions of social life, from presidential elections to the consumption of ties and cigarettes." ((Holz, Kofler and Abendroth, 1966:150) What led to the spectacular expansiveness of the commodity form in the 20th century was the new technical basis of commodity production based on the assembly line linked to the conveyor belt (Fordism). of big industry machines allowed, in terms of production, the position of the real subsumption of labor to capital, whose counterpart, in terms of social reproduction, is the manipulation with regard to the immersion of the man who works in the world of commodities. Capitalist wealth appears as an immense collection of goods whose way of being permeates social life. In fact, the idea of impregnation of social life by the commodity-form is the idea of adherence/dissemination of the commodity fetish, treated by Marx in section IV of Chapter 1 of Book I of "Capital") when he sought to reveal the secret of " fetishism which adheres to the products of labor as soon as they are produced as commodities, and which, therefore, is inseparable from the production of commodities" (Marx, 1996:199).

B. Relative surplus value and manipulation

In *History and Class Consciousness* (1923), Lukács dealt, in a pioneering way, with the social implications of capitalist reification in human activity and thought. In that classic study, when dealing with capitalist reification, the Hungarian philosopher addressed a critical aspect of the problem of manipulation. Lukács explained the nature of the social metabolism of the new capitalism that emerged with the expansion of the commodity form under the mass production of commodities (Fordism-Taylorism). Lukács linked the problem of manipulation to the predominance of relative surplus value in the dynamics of capitalist exploitation. As the form of capitalist exploitation changed, the living conditions of the workforce changed in terms of not only their relationship with the work process. with the new machines in the production process, but also with the validity of the new social metabolism based on the commodity form . Thus, a new way of organizing free time and consumption emerged, with decisive implications in terms of the subjectivity of the person-who-works.

In the 1965 interview, the old Lukács highlighted the new (and important) aspect of the problem of social manipulation. He noted that it was exploitation based on relative surplus value that allowed capitalism to raise the worker's standard of living, with profound implications on the plane of the contingent consciousness of the working class: "The exploitation of the working class increasingly passes from exploitation through absolute surplus value for that which operates through relative surplus value. This means that an increase in exploitation alongside an increase in the worker's standard of living is possible. In Marx's time there was something similar, but only in embryonic form; I'm not saying it didn't exist at all. Marx recognized, in the field of economics, and I believe he was the first to do so, relative surplus value; but he did it himself once, in a part of 'O Capital' unpublished, a very interesting observation; that is: that through absolute surplus value production is only formally subsumed under capital, so that the subsumption of production under the categories of capitalism only arises with relative surplus value, something that constitutes a specific characteristic of our epoch. (Holz, Kofler and Abendroth, 1966:152) [emphasis added].

The position of relative surplus value meant the establishment of the capitalist mode of production itself, given that production was actually subsumed under capital. Previously, under the predominance of absolute surplus value, capitalist production was only formally subsumed under capital. But the decisive point is that the old Lukács derived from the historical passage from the formal subsumption to the real subsumption of labor to capital in the plane of capitalist production, sociometabolic implications; in other words, capitalist manipulation was pointed out in an incisive way to the extent that greater exploitation corresponded, at the same time, to an increase in the wage worker's standard of living, with significant implications in terms of the contingent consciousness of the man who works. This is the problematic of the bourgeoisification of the working class. Thus, in the historical conditions of late capitalism, commodity fetishism, which hides, on the plane of contingent consciousness, the social work contained in commodity products, was raised to the nth power. The exacerbation of the commodity fetish under late capitalism constituted a social metabolism based incisively on social manipulation, that is, on the concealment - not only of capitalist exploitation - but of the centrality of social work. It is not just the fact of capitalist exploitation that is concealed in the commodity form, but the very fact that it is a product of social labor. The awareness of alienation - and the nature of alienation - change significantly, with the intense (and extensive) presence of relative surplus value and the constitution of the bourgeois social world as an "immense collection of commodities".

C. The new alienation/estrangement

Lukács makes an important observation about the concrete mutation of the problem of alienation/estrangement [Entfremdung] as the capitalist mode of production changes with the full validity of relative surplus value: "The entire problem of alienation acquires an entirely new physiognomy . At the time when Marx was writing the ' ¬*Economic and Philosophical Manuscripts* ', the alienation of the working class immediately meant oppressive work on an almost animal level. Indeed, alienation was, in a sense, synonymous with inhumanity. Precisely for this reason , the class struggle had the objective, for decades, of guaranteeing, with appropriate demands on salary and working time, the minimum of human life for the worker. The famous claim of eight hours' work put forward by the Second International it is a symptom of this class struggle." (Holz, Kofler and Abendroth, 1966:165)

In terms of the contingent consciousness of the working man, alienation in Marx's time appeared as inhumanity in the sense that the working class was subjected to oppressive work on an almost animal level. At that time, capitalist exploitation appeared, almost immediately, to the contingent consciousness of wage workers.

Furthermore, the industrial proletariat did not have access, in terms of consumption, to the commodity products of large capitalist industry. At the beginning of industrial capitalism, the "society of mass consumption" had not been constituted, the mode of social organization that hides today, in terms of commodity fetishism, the incisive dimension of capitalist exploitation. As relative surplus value became effective, there was an increase in the standard of living of an expanded portion of the salaried working class, with access by the organized proletariat to an "immense collection of goods" aimed at satisfying the new needs created by the capitalist mode of production. According to Lukács, the problem of alienation/estrangement has changed significantly, which is rephrased in other categorical terms. He says: "Absolute surplus value has not died, but simply no longer performs its role. dominant role; that role it played when Marx was writing the ' ¬Economic and Philosophical Manuscripts ' . Now, what follows from that? That a new problem appears on the horizon of the workers, that is, the problem of a life full of meaning." (Holz, Kofler and Abendroth , 1966:162)

What Lukács suggests is the organic link between the problem of manipulation due to the mass production of capitalist industry and the burning obsession with selling merchandise-products to the working class with better purchasing power, thus mobilizing marketing and propaganda apparatuses; and the problem of estrangement, which manifests itself – for example - in the problem of a life full of meaning.

D. Manipulation, estrangement and the lack of a life full of meaning

The new position of relative surplus value brought about two perverse moments in the field of subjectivity of the proletariat class: On the one hand, it increased the rate of exploitation or extraction of relative surplus value, with a reduction in relative wages . The reduction of relative wages in the 20th century is the result of the limits of trade unionism, as denounced, for example, by Rosa Luxemburg who believed that "capitalist production cannot advance a single step forward without reducing workers' participation in the social product". The reduction in workers' participation in the social product and the increase in capitalists' participation occurred through technical innovations in production, through increased labor productivity. Faced with the law of the tendency of relative wages to fall , considered by her to be a "completely invisible power, a simply mechanical action of competition and commodity production", which leaves workers with an ever smaller portion of the social wealth produced, the unions could do nothing to do. The unions could only take care of the "visible attack of the capitalists against the workers", that is, the reductions in real wages, which lower the standard of living of the working class. Faced with the invisible fall in relative wages, they would feel powerless: "The fight against the fall in relative wages is no longer a struggle that takes place in the field of the mercantile economy, but rather a revolutionary, subversive assault against the existence of this economy, It is the socialist movement of the proletariat." (Rosdolsky , 2001)

In the last half of the twentieth century, late capitalism led to the exacerbation of relative surplus value extraction due to the admirable technological innovations that increased, in an unprecedented way, the productivity of social labor and the power of capital. On the other hand, the increase in the extraction of surplus value allowed the relative increase in the standard of living of expressive contingents of the proletariat, which now had access to an immense collection of products-commodities in order to satisfy new necessary needs of metropolitan life. The dissemination of the commodity form to an unprecedented extent, with the fetish of the commodity pervading social life, more candidly clouded the necessary class consciousness. Thus, according to Lukács, under manipulative capitalism (or late capitalism), the problem of alienation/estrangement was replaced, in a broad and burning way, on another existential level, through the problem of the lack of a full meaning life. The world full of commodities is the world full of manipulations that penetrate not only the pores of production, but also of consumption and social reproduction.

Thus, if, on the one hand, the perception of capitalist exploitation and the problem of alienation in the original sense exposed by Marx in the "Manuscripts of 1844", tended to fade; on the other hand, they incisively pose, in line with the old Lukács, the problem of estrangement as the problem of a life full of meaning (for example, the Austrian psychoanalyst Viktor Frankl stressed that the crucial problem of our time is the problem of the search for the meaning of life) (Frankl, 2005). The structural change in the character of alienation posed, in a burning way, at the height of affluent capitalism (in 1968), new demands on the level of class struggle . Lukács says: "The class struggle ¬in the time of absolute surplus value was aimed at creating the objective conditions indispensable to a life of this kind. Today, with a five-day week and an adequate salary, the indispensable conditions for a life full of meaning may already exist . But a new problem arises: that manipulation that goes from buying cigarettes to presidential elections erects a barrier inside individuals between their existence and a life rich in meaning. In effect, the manipulation of consumption does not consist, as is officially intended, in wanting to exhaustively inform consumers about which is the best refrigerator or the best razor; what is at stake is the question of control of consciousness . I will give just one example, the 'type' Gauloises: a man with an active and masculine appearance is presented, who is distinguished because he smokes Gauloises cigarettes. Or again, I see in an advertising photo, I don't know if it's a soap or a shaving cream, a young man harassed by two beautiful girls because of the erotic attraction that a certain perfume exerts on them" (Holz, Kofler and Abendroth, 1966 : p.167).

Lukács, adopting the historical-ontological perspective, makes the intimate connection between relative surplus value and manipulation in the sense that exploitation by relative surplus value provided, to an organized contingent of the working class, a five-day week and adequate salary, that is that is, indispensable objective conditions for a life full of meaning. Objectively, the proletariat today has the material conditions for a life full of meaning, which, however, does not take place, due to the social manipulation that permeates bourgeois life. The capitalism of the great industry of mass production tends, in the words of the Hungarian philosopher, to erect, inside the individuals, "a barrier between their existence and a life rich in meaning". The enjoyment of life is reduced to the enjoyment of alienated consumption. The fleeting desire for commodity consumption is incapable of giving meaning to life. This is the meaning of estrangement from Lukacs' perspective: the mismatch between the existence of individuals and a *life full of meaning* .

In a way, for Lukács, the problem of estrangement concerns the issue of controlling consciousness , a key target of the manipulation of consumption aimed at selling goods and achieving surplus value . Manipulation arises within individuals whose desire for consumption is instilled by marketing and advertising apparatuses, as an end in itself. Lukács says: "Because of this manipulation, the worker, the man who works, is removed from the problem of how he could transform his free time into otium, because consumption is instilled in him in the form of a superabundance of life with a purpose in itself. , just as in the twelve-hour working day life was dictatorially dominated by work" (Holz, Kofler and Abendroth, 1966:170).

In several passages of his interview, Lukács called the worker or salaried worker the "man who works", an expression that explains what is, in fact, today, under the crossfire of manipulative capitalism: the man or the human-generic nucleus of salaried workers. Before being salaried workers, we are effectively men who work. Thus, the word "man" in the sense of the generic human being is highlighted. This is the radical meaning of Lukács' humanist Marxism (radical in the sense of going to the roots, and the root is man himself).

D. FREE TIME AND *OTIUM*

In developed capitalist countries, in 1965, the height of affluent capitalism, a significant portion of the proletariat class enjoyed a five--day week and an adequate salary, which guaranteed a better standard of living compared to the industrial proletarians of the 19th century . For the old Lukács, what arises, under the conditions of the "Welfare State", is the problem of how to transform free time into otium (idleness) or time freed from the manipulation of capital; finally, life time as a field of human development, which does not immediately occur with the reduction of the working day.

The production of relative surplus value created the objective bases for the human release of work as an exclusive activity. Although the man who works today has more time freed from strange work, it does not mean that the available time is free time in the sense of creative leisure. In fact, for Lukács, the problem is how to transform liberated time into free time; or free time in otium . Under manipulative capitalism, free time from alienated work has become mere manipulated consumption time. Thus, the problem of manipulation, which Lukács placed as intrinsic to the capitalism of large industry, displaced the question of the struggle for the reduction of the working day to the question of the transformation of free time into otium (the crisis of late capitalism and the historical era of global capitalism with the sociometabolism of barbarism altered this equation of manipulation: the precariousness of work effectively means the transformation of free time or even otium space into estranged work time).

Insofar as bourgeois society has become at that time an immense collection of commodities, the relative liberation of the working man from the alienation of alien labor only places him at the mercy of another master: the Commodity. For Lukács, although necessary, the struggle to reduce the working day is not enough to create the material bases for the social emancipation of the proletariat. Finally, from the Lukacsian point of view, at the height of late capitalism, more than ever, the need to form human subjects capable of transforming free time into otium was placed, breaking with the eagerness instilled by the logic of merchandise to transform free time into consumption time as an end in itself. However, in our days, the precariousness of work that characterizes global capitalism, the man who works is at the mercy of himself as a Commodity, with the otium space and the time freed by the productivity of work, interverted in estranged work time, self-employment or even survivalism (Han, 2020:33).

But let's return to Lukács' reflection at the height of late capitalism (1965). If the reduction of the working day and the expansion of the time freed from strange work had to occur through a political act, the transformation of free time into otium, or rather, of available time into free time in the full sense of the word, implied a extra-parliamentary act, that is, the formation of human subjects capable of enjoying creative leisure, breaking with the sociometabolism of capital . Ultimately, individuals may simply not know what to do with their free time. It was in this sense that Lukács made in "History and Class

Consciousness" (1923), the critique of contemplative men, individuals created by the cultural and entertainment industry society, men and women (de)formed to merely contemplate the spectacular world of commodities.

E. Strange consumption and human-generic desubjectivation

Lukács identified manipulation as occurring intensively in the sphere of consumption that transformed the superabundance of life in the sense of an immense collection of goods to be consumed, as an end in itself. Thus, from a means of livelihood, consumption becomes an end in itself (consumerism), which is the proper meaning – according to Lukács – of alienation . Before, it occurred (and occurs) in strange work , and today, he says, also in strange consumption . Thus, the sphere of social alienation was expanded.

By becoming an end in itself, consumption becomes consumerism. Strictly speaking, bourgeois society is not a "consumer society", but a "consumer society". Another thing: ideology wants us to believe that we consume things that we actually buy. Now, buying is not an action governed by necessary needs, but an economic act with social implications. Says Jurandir Freire Costa: "Buying has become equivalent to consuming because the rhythm of production of goods obliges us to discard them after a brief use. Consumption is a metaphor that alludes to the speed with which we acquire new objects and render old ones useless [...] After the great technological and economic revolutions, capitalist production, in order to be sold, had and has to be sold in a continuous flow. Individuals, therefore, have to buy the commodities so that the profit machine does not stop". However, he asks himself: why do individuals allow themselves to be seduced by merchandise advertising? He suggests that the habit of consumerism meets real psychosocial needs, that is, individuals allow themselves to be persuaded by advertising because, to a certain extent, they find in the possession of industrial objects a means of personal fulfillment. This aspiration to personal fulfillment – or what Lukács suggests as having a life full of meaning – is the reason for the yearning for "objects of consumption". Costa observes that the new morality of work and the new morality of pleasure contribute to the production of the desire to consume (Costa, 2004). Another thing: Juliet B. Schor correctly uses the appropriate word in the title of her thought-provoking book ("Born to buy] : it is not about "Born to consume", but rather, "Born to buy" .

In late bourgeois society, the sphere of consumption has expanded, incorporating not only commodity products that satisfy the needs of the stomach, but, as Marx noted, the needs of fantasy. The best example is the cultural industry that involves men and women in capital society; and by the way, not just workers and employees, but all human beings, including (and especially) young people and children who still do not work. Due to the fetishism of merchandise, the condition of consumers hides the condition of producers from men who work, becoming today, broader than the condition of salaried workers. Therefore, the problem of manipulation, or the problem of a life full of meaning, appears as a universal problem that involves not only workers and employees, but all individuals at the mercy of the fetishized implications of the aesthetics of the commodity . As we have seen, Lukács pointed out that in manipulative capitalism in its ascendant phase, " consumption is instilled in it in the form of an overabundance of life with a purpose in itself ." We can draw some conclusions from this statement by old Lukács:

FIRST, manipulation appears as a reductive instillation that presents the image of the spectacular world of commodities, with its "superabundance of life", as an end in itself. The best example is the case of the admirable world of shopping malls , whose spectacular architecture aims to expose the world of merchandise as the only possible world.

SECONDLY, manipulation appears as a (de) formative process or process of strange subjectivation, which (de)constitutes human personalities, or rather, human subjectivities reduced to their own abstraction, in the same sense of the reduction carried out by the validity of the abstract work. It is what we can call "abstract individualities". Therefore, the spaces of consumption under manipulative capitalism appear as spaces of commodity pedagogy , where men and women, children, young people, adults and the elderly are educated, surreptitiously, to reduce the enjoyment of life to the delight of consumerism. The act of living becomes the mere act of consuming. In this way, we can say, from Lukács, that the social metabolism of the capital. under manipulative capitalism, it involves a twofold process:

On the one hand, the social metabolism of capital is a process of human-generic desubjectivation and, consequently, a process of class desubjectivation in the sense of corroding the historical subject capable of making history; on the other hand, the social metabolism of capital is a process of fetishized subjectivation in the sense of forming "abstract human individualities" "affected by negation". That is, as life is reduced to consumerism, an acute human frustration opens up within personal class individualities, not only with regard to the "desire for meaning" (using Viktor Frankl's expression), but with regard to the satisfaction of "radical needs" posed, objectively, by the human-generic civilizing process.

Manipulation is the social phenomenon that arises, in terms of production and social reproduction, with capital's inability to deal with the disruption of human personality due to the burning sociometabolic contradictions of the commodity producing system. By being incapable of providing a life full of meaning, capital in its most developed historical form (global capitalism) finds itself facing irremediable structural limits. Albert Camus once remarked, "There is only one truly serious problem, and that is . . . establishing whether or not life is worth living." (Camus,1955). Psychiatrist Viktor Frankl , in 1949, introduced the concept of "desire for meaning" to deal with a problem of our historical time - the lack of a life full of meaning - which leads human individuals to personal drift. He says: "In some cases, the frustration of the desire for meaning played a relevant role as an etiological factor in giving rise to neurosis or suicide attempts.". And further on he stresses: "Man's search for a meaning for life is, obviously, a worldwide phenomenon." (Frankl , 2006). However, Frankl 's diagnosis is not complete: the thirst for meaning (which is another book title by Frank, 2003) that he finds to be a worldwide phenomenon and the pathology of our time, is a product of manipulative capitalism (Lukács) and the strange control of the social metabolism (Mészáros), that is, of the capital that, in this stage of civilizing development, makes its objective contradictions exhaustively explicit.

In this way, it can be said that the core of manipulation as an instillation of the reductive culture of consumption as an end in itself, hides the sinister operation of de-effectiveness of the generic being of man , insofar as man assumes the position of mere passive adaptation to the spectacular environment of the goods. It is not about the death of the human subject, as postmodern metaphysics supposes, but the opening of the "crack" of intimate contradictions within the personal class individualities. To the same extent that they are intensely manipulated, men and women are instigated, in and for themselves, to respond to their human frustrations, whether in terms of the "desire for meaning" (Viktor Frankl), or in terms of "radical needs" " (Agnes Heller). The inability to give satisfactory answers is what leads men and women to physical and mental illness in multiple ways.

F. SOCIALISM AND HUMANIZATION OF WORK

Estrangement permeates not only the act of consumption, but the capitalist work process in its essential core. Labor, as Marx noted, always remains, necessarily, the 'realm of necessity'. For Lukács, the development of socialism aims precisely at giving humanly adequate forms to work and the development of humanity (a burning problem in the era of historical decay of capital with the precariousness of work). Lukács noted that Marx, in the "Critique of the Gotha Programme", asserted that, one of the conditions for communism is that work becomes a vital need for man. Finally, socialism must seek to humanize the realm of necessity.

Under manipulative capitalism, work acquired intimately inhuman forms, with a view to manipulation towards the control of consciousness – and worse, with the structural crisis of capital, the precariousness of work accentuated the dimension of dehumanization of work, extending it to the free space of time. This is what we call "capturing" the subjectivity of the man who works for capital (Alves, 2007). The destructive production of capital has become a social totality. It is in this sense that Lukács says (in 1965): "Today there is a science of work and a psychological assistance for the worker, but they aim to make the existing capitalist technology acceptable to him through manipulation, and do not serve to create, on the contrary, a technology capable of transforming work into a experience worthy of being lived by the worker" (Holz, Kofler and Abendroth, 1966: p.168). Even with technical-scientific progress, work as an ineradicable realm of necessity has not become, as the Hungarian philosopher observed, "an experience worthy of being lived by the worker".

On the contrary, the working man still wants to escape from it, considering that it does not find elements of human dignity in it. And today, faced with the logic of survivalism and the precariousness of wage statutes, the man who works is cornered by the full domain of strange work. The strange work under the social logic of systemic toyotism (Alves, 2001), destroys life in the sense of life as a field of human development. This is what the statistics on illnesses in the world of work attest today, due to the pressure for greater productivity and achievement of goals, with inhuman and humanly impossible goals. In fact, no matter how much one tries to "humanize" work environments, capitalist work is still strange work in the sense of being work for someone else, the strange other, the capitalist; work alienated from the purposes of human-generic fruition of working men and women.

The social world of late capitalism, according to Lukács, is marked by estrangement in its multiple dimensions. Lukács highlighted the estrangement at work , considering that, for him, work remains an unworthy experience for the man who works. But as we have seen, Lukács also highlighted the strangeness of consumption : freed from working time, individuals do not find a life full of meaning. In addition to instances of work and consumption, estrangement (and manipulation) permeates other instances of social life, such as politics and culture – an essential dimension in the formation of human genericity.

In the case of the sphere of consumption, the impossibility of capital at the height of late capitalism in the mid-1960s - to transform free time into otium , is the greatest demonstration that, as Lukács observes, "this manipulation is contrary to properly human interests". With manipulative capitalism, the power of ideology has emerged with unprecedented vigor . In view of this, there is the political need for ideological work, in the sense of socialist ideology, capable of making it clearer how the manipulation of the ideological apparatuses of capital is contrary to properly human interests. Lukács stressed that manipulation is not omnipotent.

For example, he observed: "For twenty years (around 1948), there has been a permanent struggle in haute Couture over the fact that it, as a manipulation of women's clothing, wants to introduce long skirts anyway. It is clear that this happens because the profit of the textile industry would be greater in this case. Fashion, which, as they say, is omnipotent, fails, however, on this point. Twenty years ago, in Paris, at the big fashion shows, people continued to prophesy the length of skirts; however, at this point, women defend their rights, because long skirts are not suitable for work or going up on a crowded train" (Holz, Kofler and Abendroth, 1966:170).

What was at stake at that time (and today in the era of barbaric sociometabolism), more than ever, are human interests in the sense of human genericity and not just the class interests in and for themselves of the proletariat. Finally, according to the old Lukács, in these new historical circumstances of ideological crisis of the global system of capital, the need arises not only for consciousness in and for itself of the proletariat, but for the class consciousness of the proletariat beyond itself. (Mészáros, 2008:80-81).

4

Estrangement as a universal fact

It is interesting to resume the discussion on the concept of estrangement according to the old Lukács. In a passage from the 1965 interview, when dealing with the manipulation process, he makes a very interesting observation: "[...] it is truly a process that no longer has the working class as its only point of reference; in this respect, that is, in terms of relative surplus value and manipulation, even the intellectual strata and the entire bourgeoisie are equally subject to capitalism and its manipulations, no less than the working class. It is therefore a question of awakening the true autonomy of the personality , and for this the economic development carried out up to the present moment has created the necessary conditions" (Holz, Kofler and Abendroth, 1966:165).

Thus, under manipulative capitalism, it is not just the working class that is subject to the miseries of manipulation, but even the intellectual layer and the entire bourgeoisie are subject to estrangement that diminishes the autonomy of the personality. The universal condition of estrangement, which today, more than ever, involves humanity, is what we call the "proletarian condition", an existential condition of the human race that is subsumed and subaltern to the sociometabolism of capital (Alves, 2009)

It is clear that the bourgeoisie, dwarfed by estrangement, does not have the political-ideological capacity to promote the negation of negation . They are incapable of true class consciousness "beyond themselves". On the contrary, the bourgeoisie and its social personas , to the extent that they experience estrangement as positivity , are condemned to the tragic torment of being, at the same time, agents (and victims) of the miseries of capital manipulation.

In conditions of the advanced stage of the civilizing process of capital, the problem of manipulation that reached its height with late capitalism, acquired a problematic content of a new type. Lukács observed that the amount of work necessary for the physical reproduction of man it has steadily diminished, which means that, for all men, the necessary space for a socially human existence can be found today more than at any other time. This reduction of the natural barriers that constrain the human species, even taking place under the sociometabolic system of capital, is the "civilizing process of capital". It is clear that the reduction of natural barriers, the reduction of the amount of work necessary for the physical reproduction of man, does not mean, in and for itself, the social emancipation of work, but only the explanation of its assumptions and necessary objectives frustrated by the relationship -capital. According to Lukács, a historical moment like this happened in an economically limited way, with the pioneers of civilization, when, for example, in Athens, "slavery freed a privileged layer from work, thus allowing the birth of the great Athenian culture". As in Ancient Greece, slavery allowed the birth of universal civilizing values, under the late West, the development of the machine system, in what it represents of reducing natural barriers, would allow, as long as the capital-relation was abolished, a new civilization leap, the development of socialism. The new civilizational leap, socialism as a world system, means not only the establishment of a new way of controlling the social metabolism, but the salvation of humanity from its irremediable extinction by capital. In this way, we can say that socialism becomes an imposed historical necessity, not by the depletion of the civilizing capacity of capital, but rather by the burning socio-metabolic contradictions that emerge within the civilization of capital and that can lead to the extinction of humanity .

Lukács observed that it is undeniable that there are social strata of the proletariat for which the old categories of capitalism are still valid in terms of living standards, and, according to him, "it is naturally a great task to prepare for their disappearance and to demand that the worker another level of life". It is possible, within late capitalism, to improve the standard of living of poor contingents of the proletariat who still did not have adequate wages and degrading working conditions. But, noted Lukács, there is no doubt that, for a large mass of salaried workers, objective conditions were created capable of making possible a life free and adequate to human requirements. For this reason, according to Lukacs, "it is necessary to undertake a broad discussion on the current forms of alienation ". In fact, what Lukács indicates is the intensification of the objective and subjective historical contradiction that is intrinsic to the civilizing process of capital, the contradiction between material social conditions capable, in and for themselves, of making possible a life free and adequate to human demands. ; and the strange mode of control of capital's social metabolism, based on the hierarchical division of labor and private ownership of the means of production, today, more and more concentrated than ever in world oligopolies. The irremediable frustration of the objective possibilities of human-generic development and the effective non-realization of the promises contained in the material conditions opened by the civilizing process, make up the nature of the phenomenon of estrangement. Here is how the Hungarian philosopher exposes in the "Ontology of Social Being", in simple terms, the problem of estrangement: "The development of productive forces is necessarily also the development of human capacity, but – and here the problem of estrangement practically emerges – the development of human capacity does not necessarily produce the [development] of the human personality . On the contrary: precisely by enhancing unique capabilities, it can disfigure, demean, etc., the personality of man" (Lukács, 2013:561) [emphasis added]

The development of productive forces in the sense of the civilizing process as a reduction of natural barriers means the development of human capacity. However, how would the development of human capabilities be expressed ?

First, by increasing the productivity of human labor and mastering space-time and natural forces. This is what happened in the last centuries of industrial capitalism with the development of science and technology. The progress of science and technique as technology is an unquestionable fact of the civilization of capital. This is the instrumental sense of the concept of development of the productive forces.

Second, the development of human capacity means, to the same extent, the development of human-social skills capable of promoting the human development of men. Which would imply conceiving man as a productive force not only in the instrumental sense, but in the sense of the affirmation and denial of human sociability, even if it is as a denied assumption, as occurs under the sociometabolic system of capital. It is unquestionable that, in the last centuries of the civilization of capital, an individuation process took place that can be conceived as a development of the human capacity of men. For example, new modes of cooperation and division of labor mean new ways of organizing socio-human skills capable of boosting the productive forces of social labor, which are productive forces of capital. Therefore, nowadays, capital managers know that the increase of the productive forces of social work implies not only investing in technology (hardware or software), but in management/manipulation of human abilities/subjectivities (humanware).

Capital as a "living contradiction" operates an inversion/perversion of the development of productive forces as a development of human capacity. The problem of estrangement is at the heart of capital's "living contradiction". Here's how it looks:

First, the technologization of the sciences , which surrender to the instrumentality of the interests of capital production; technology as the social form of capital imprints the mark of manipulation on the foundation of scientific undertakings. Which explains the voracious criticism that the last Lukács made of neopositivism as an ideology of the manipulated world of capital;

According to Human (de)formation of resources for management/manipulation of production and social reproduction. There is a tenuous (and perverse) line of continuity between new management methods that promise more productivity in companies and the positive discourse of self-help literature that promises self-satisfaction /personal fulfillment.

The sociometabolism of barbarism that emerges with the structural crisis of capital means the gradual corrosion of human capacities in the sense of making them effective in their human-generic dimension. This is the "root" of the sociability crisis. The paradox of "capturing" the subjectivity of work is that effectively subjectivity cannot be "captured". In this case, there is a perverse contradiction between objectively realized human capacities, in terms of technical and scientific basis; and subjectively deactivated , in the sense of practical-sensitive appropriation of them by the men who work.

The development of (in)capabilities composes the core contradiction between posited objective possibilities , an objectivity that is irremediably subjectively mediated, and a derealization effected within the very sociometabolism of capital. Lukács stressed that the development of human capacity under capital does not necessarily produce the development of human personality. The development of men and women as human subjects or the human becoming of men does not in itself depend on scientific-technological development. On the contrary, the development of human capabilities, both technical capabilities interverted into technological (in)capabilities, and training capabilities interverted in deformative manipulations , under the social world of capital, they tend to disfigure, demean, etc., the personality of the working man. The disfiguration and debasement of the human personality occurs as the development of human capacities enhances, not the human-generic capacities, but the singular capacities of the man who works . This is the idea of forming personalities immersed in particularisms or social barbarism as we conceive it.

Both the technological devices that organize the space-time of capital production and reproduction, as well as the management/manipulation resources of the subjectivity of the working man, contribute to the (de)formation of the human personality through the cultivation of unique capacities (or particularists) of human individualities. It is interesting that many of the technological resources, whether high-tech gadgets or even urban equipment that organize our bourgeois lifestyle, contribute to the formation of unique capacities or selfish-particularist dispositions of individuals. The best example is the privileging of automobiles to the detriment of public transport in urban centers and the organization of urban spaces as a function of this unique capacity for spatial locomotion. Another fact of this formation of unique capabilities as a way of deforming the generic being of man is the degradation of public spaces and forms of collective sociability).

Finally, Lukács, in the last decade of his life, placed important elements for us to reflect on the problem of social barbarism that characterizes our historical time, that is, the perverse implication of the sociometabolism of barbarism that, in a contradictory way, disables man as a generic being , enhancing his unique capabilities, deforming him as a social being within a society that is increasingly social in an objective sense. This potentialization of singular capacities to the detriment of human-generic capacities is explained in the very corrosion of the ideal of collectivity as a space for the development of social individualities. In fact, the problem of estrangement is the excruciating contradiction of capital's civilizing process.

Referências

ALVES, Giovanni (2009) *A condição de proletariedade*, Editora Praxis: Bauru.

_____(2011) *Trabalho e subjetividade: O espírito do toyotismo na era do capitalismo manipulatório.* Boitempo editorial: São Paulo.

COSTA, Jurandir Freire (2004) "Perspectivas da juventude na sociedade de mercado" In NOVAES, Regina e VANUCCHI, Paulo (Org.) *Juventude e Sociedade – Trabalho, Educação, Cultura e Participação.* Instituto Cidadania/Fundação Perseu Abramo, São Paulo.

FRANKL, Viktor E. (2005) *Um sentido para a vida: Psicoterapia e Humanismo*, Idéias e Letras, São Paulo.

_____ (2003) *Sede de Sentido*, Quadrante, São Paulo.

_____ (2018) *O duplo negativo do capital: Ensaios sobre a crise do capitalismo global.* Bauru: Projeto editorial Praxis.

LUKÁCS, György (2013) *Para uma ontologia do ser social,* volume II, São Paulo: Boitempo editorial.

LUKÁCS, György (2020) *Essenciais são os livros não escritos: Ultimas entrevistas (1966-1971).* São Paulo: Boitempo editorial.

LUKÁCS, György (2007). "As bases ontológicas do pensamento e da atividade do homem" In LUKÁCS, György. *O jovem Marx e outros escritos de filosofia*. Editora UFRJ, Rio de Janeiro.

_____(1999) *Pensamento Vivido – Autobiografia em diálogo*. Ad Hominam/Editora UFV, Viçosa.

LOJKINE, Jean (1995) *A revolução informacional*. São Paulo: Cortez.

HAN, Byung-Chul (2020) *Sociedade paliativa/A dor hoje*. Rio de Janeiro: Editora Vozes.

HOLZ, H., KOFLER, L. e ABENDROTH, W. (1969) *Conversando com Lukács*, Paz e Terra, Rio de Janeiro.

MARX, Karl (1996) *O Capital: Critica da economia política*, Livro 1, Tomo I, Editora Nova Cultural, São Paulo.

MÉSZÁROS, István (2006). *A teoria da alienação em Marx*. Editora Boitempo, São Paulo.

_____(2008) *Filosofia, Ideologia e Ciência Social*. Editora Boitempo, São Paulo.

_____(2002) *Para além do capital: Rumo a uma teoria da transição*. São Paulo: Boitempo editorial.

NOZAKI, Hajime Takeuchi (2021) *A crise do capital em Marx: O debate contemporâneo entre os marxistas*. Juiz de Fora: Editora UFJF.

ROSDOLSKY, Roman (2001) *Gênese e estrutura de O capital de Karl Marx*. Contraponto: Rio de Janeiro.

SCHOR, Juliet B. (2009) *Nascidos para comprar – Uma leitura essencial para orientarmos nossas crianças na era do consumismo*. Gente Editora, São Paulo.

TERTULIAN, Nicola (2007) "El pensamiento del último Lukács" In In VEDDA, Miguel e INFRANCA, Antonino (Org.) *György Lukács – Ética, Estética y Ontologia*, Ediciones Colihue Universidad, Buenos Aires.

_____(2008) *Gyorgy Lukács: Etapas de seu pensamento estético*. São Paulo: editora Unesp.

ABOUT THE AUTHOR

Giovanni Alves is an associate professor at the São Paulo State University (UNESP, Marília/SP, Brazil). He is a postdoctoral fellow at the Centro de Estudos Sociais (CES) at the University of Coimbra (Portugal); and the Complutense University of Madrid (UCM). He is author of "Work and subjectivity" (Boitempo editorial, 2011); "Dimensions of precarious work: Essays on the sociology of work" (Praxis, 2013); "The double negative of capital: Essays on the crisis of global capitalism" (Praxis, 2018) and "Aged work" (Praxis, 2021), among other books and articles in the area of work, trade unionism, productive restructuring, precarious work and workers' health.